Picasso' Trousers

Nicholas Allan

RED FOX

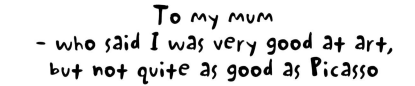

To my mum
– who said I was very good at art,
but not quite as good as Picasso

PICASSO'S TROUSERS

A RED FOX BOOK
978 0 099 49536 9
First published in Great Britain by Hutchinson,
an imprint of Random House Children's Publisher UK
A Random House Group Company

Hutchinson edition published 2011
Red Fox edition published 2012

Copyright © Nicholas Allan, 2011

1 3 5 7 9 10 8 6 4 2

The Soup, 1902 (oil on canvas) by Picasso, Pablo (1881-1973) Art Gallery of Ontario, Toronto, Canada/ Gift of Margaret Dunlap Crang, 1983/ The Bridgeman Art Library Nationality / copyright status: Spanish / in copyright until 2054 © Succession Picasso/DACS 2011

The Acrobat Family, 1905 (gouache on paper) by Picasso, Pablo (1881-1973) Goteborgs Konstmuseum, Sweden/ Giraudon/ The Bridgeman Art Library Nationality / copyright status: Spanish / in copyright until 2054 © Succession Picasso/DACS 2011

The Artist's Son in a Harlequin Costume by Picasso, Pablo (1881-1973) Galerie Daniel Malingue, Paris, France/ The Bridgeman Art Library Nationality / copyright status: Spanish / in copyright until 2054 © Succession Picasso/DACS 2011

Maria Picasso Lopez, The Artist's Mother, 1896 (pastel on paper) by Picasso, Pablo (1881-1973) Museo Picasso, Barcelona, Spain/ Giraudon/ The Bridgeman Art Library Nationality / copyright status: Spanish / in copyright until 2054 © Succession Picasso/DACS 2011

Buste de Femme, 19th November, 1936 (oil on canvas) by Picasso, Pablo (1881-1973) Private Collection/ Giraudon/ The Bridgeman Art Library Nationality / copyright status: Spanish / in copyright until 2054 © Succession Picasso/DACS 2011

Jacqueline naked in an armchair, 7th June 1964 II (oil on canvas) by Picasso, Pablo (1881-1973) Private Collection/ The Bridgeman Art Library Nationality / copyright status: Spanish / in copyright until 2054 © Succession Picasso/DACS 2011

Portrait of Dora Maar (1907-97) 1st October 1937 (oil on canvas) by Picasso, Pablo (1881-1973) Musee Picasso, Paris, France/ Giraudon/ The Bridgeman Art Library Nationality / copyright status: Spanish / in copyright until 2054 © Succession Picasso/DACS 2011

Bull's Head, Pablo Picasso © Succession Picasso – Gestion droits d'auteur. Musée Picasso, Paris; © RMN/ © Béatrice Hatala © Succession Picasso/DACS 2011

Seated Nude, 1906 (oil on canvas) by Picasso, Pablo (1881-1973) Narodni Galerie, Prague, Czech Republic/ The Bridgeman Art Library Nationality / copyright status: Spanish / in copyright until 2054 © Succession Picasso/DACS 2011

Father Christmas, 1959 by Picasso, Pablo (1881-1973) Musee d'Art et d'Histoire, Saint-Denis, France/ The Bridgeman Art Library Nationality / copyright status: Spanish / in copyright until 2054 © Succession Picasso/DACS 2011

Dove, 1961 (pastel on paper) by Picasso, Pablo (1881-1973) Private Collection/ Peter Willi/ The Bridgeman Art Library Nationality / copyright status: Spanish / in copyright until 2054 © Succession Picasso/DACS 2011

RANDOM HOUSE CHILDREN'S BOOKS
61–63 Uxbridge Road, London W5 5SA

www.kidsatrandomhouse.co.uk
www.nicholasallan.co.uk

Addresses for companies within The Random House Group Limited can be found at:
www.randomhouse.co.uk/offices.htm

THE RANDOM HOUSE GROUP Limited Reg. No. 954009

A CIP catalogue record for this book is available from the British Library.

Printed in China

The Random House Group Limited supports the Forest Stewardship Council® (FSC®), the leading international forest certification organization. Our books carrying the FSC label are printed on FSC®-certified paper. FSC is the only forest certification scheme endorsed by the leading environmental organizations, including Greenpeace. Our paper procurement policy can be found at www.randomhouse.co.uk/environment.

MIX
Paper from
responsible sources
FSC® C104723

Picasso was an artist. When he was young he wanted to go to Paris to paint.

"NO! NO! NO! Picasso!"

said his dad.

But Picasso said . . .

Vive La France!

Vive Paris!

When he got to Paris he painted many pictures. He liked **BLUE** so he decided to paint pictures all blue.
"You can't paint **ALL BLUE** pictures," they said.

"NO! NO! NO! Picasso!"

But Picasso said . . .

LIFT ←

and PINK
ones too!

Picasso was very good at faces.

He liked painting faces from the **FRONT** and from the **SIDE**.

So he decided to paint a face from the front and the side, **ALL AT THE SAME TIME!**

"You can't paint a face from the front and the side **ALL AT THE SAME TIME!**" they said.

"NO! NO! NO! Picasso!"

But Picasso said . . .

FRONT

FRONT and SIDE!

"YES!"

Soon Picasso left Paris and went to the South of France where the colours were **BEAUTIFUL.**

Picasso liked to make **ART** out of anything. So he thought he'd make some **ART** out of bike bits.

"BIKE BITS?" they said. "You can't make ART out of BIKE BITS! NO! NO! NO! Picasso!"

But Picasso said . . .

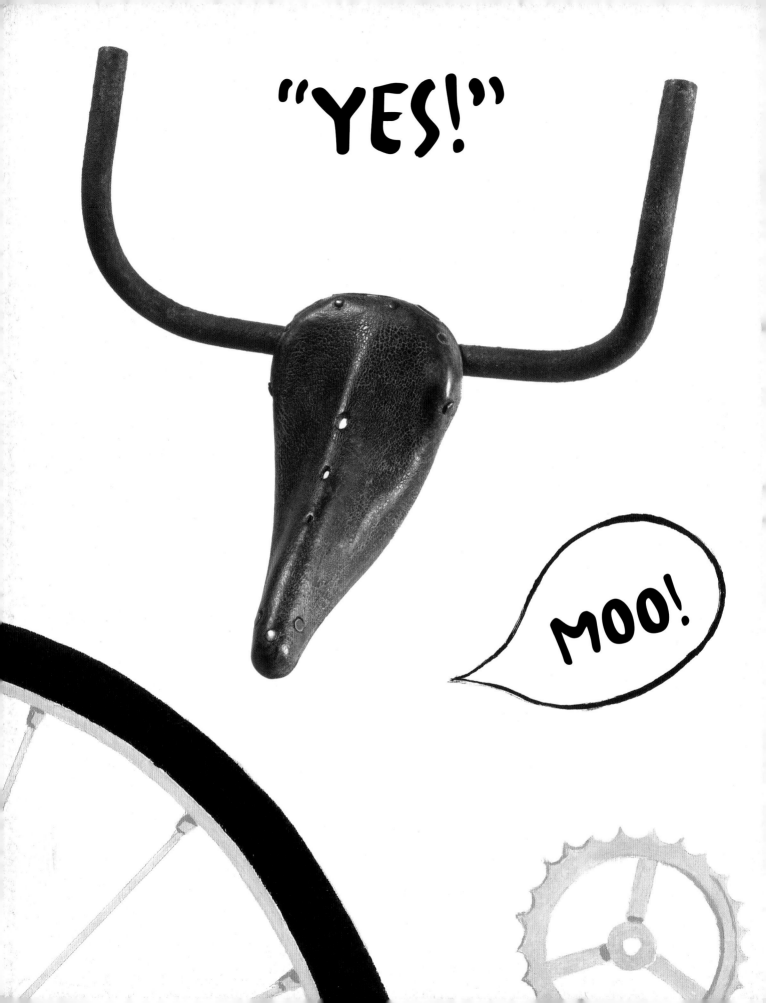

Picasso liked heavy things. But when he painted them they never looked heavy enough — so he decided to paint them heavier.

"But you can't paint

HEAVINESS!"

"NO! NO! NO! Picasso!"

But Picasso said . . .

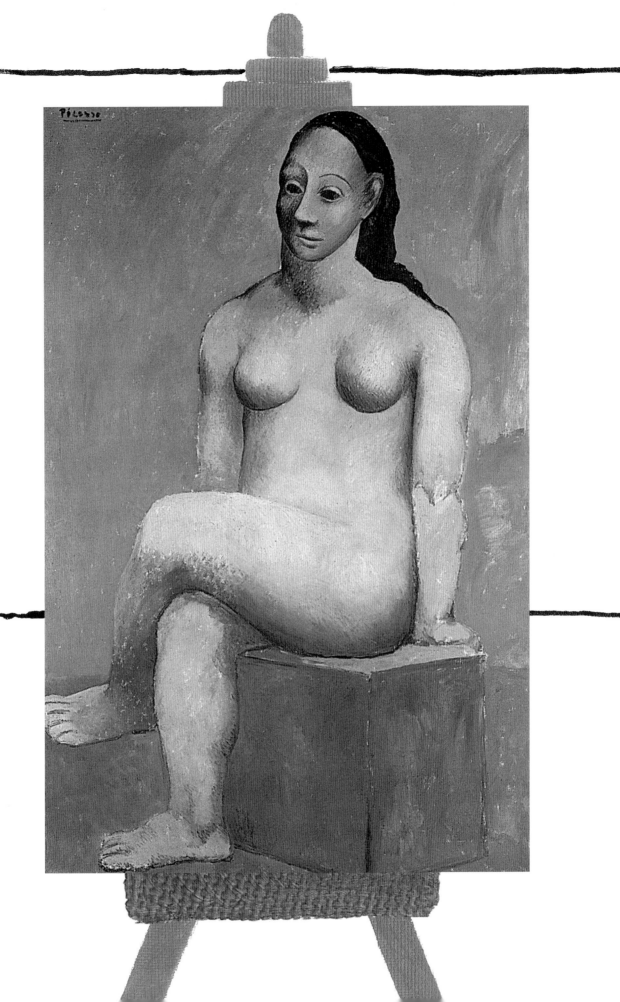

Picasso became the fastest drawer in the west.

"You can't draw in 30 seconds!" they said.

"NO! NO! N- "

"YES!"

said Picasso

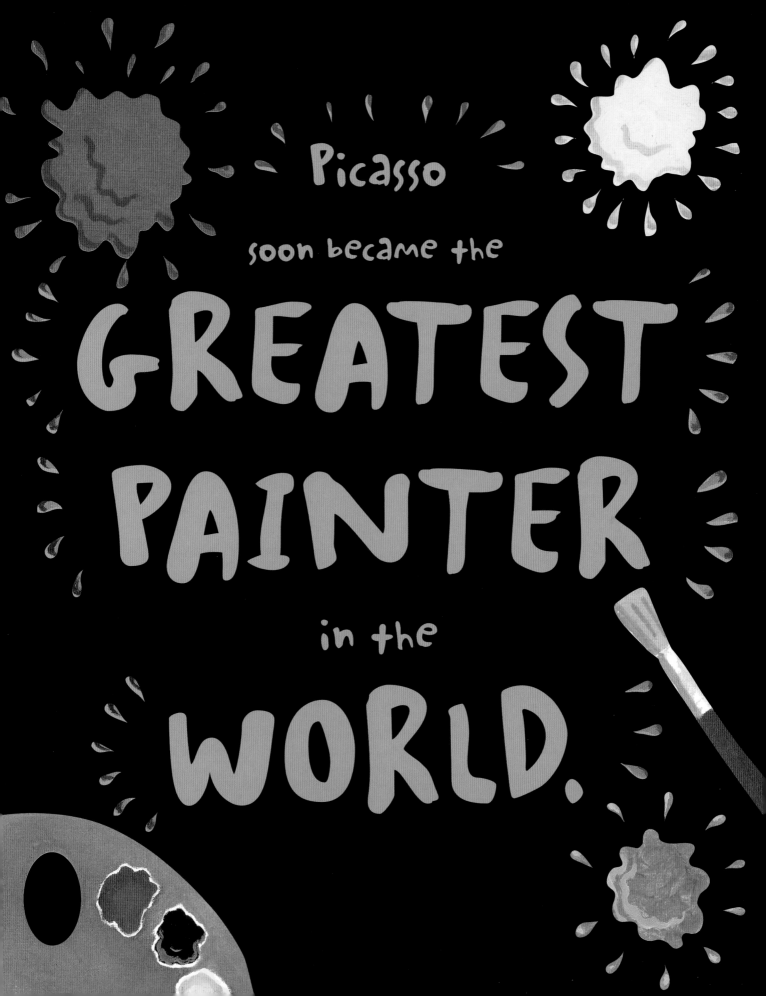

Picasso

soon became the

GREATEST

PAINTER

in the

WORLD.

And he wanted to be the BEST DRESSED painter in the world.

So he decided to buy some new trousers to match his stripy shirt. But all the stripes went the wrong way.

"You can't have stripes the OTHER way!" they said. "They'll make you look short and fat."

"NO! NO! NO! Picasso!"

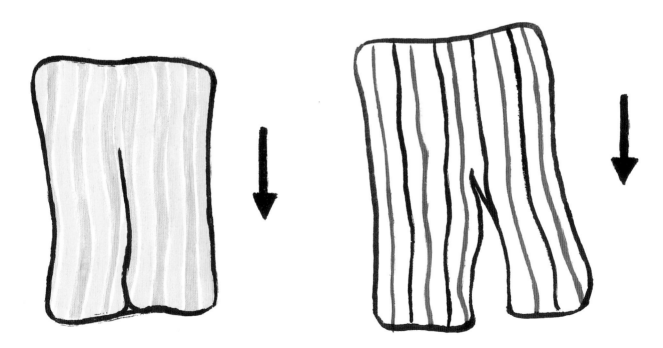

said Picasso.

"No! No! No!"

But Picasso said . . .

lift here

After this picture, Picasso, with his pal Braque, started doing cubist paintings. The paintings showed people and objects — like mandolins and bowls of fruit — from all different sides. It was as if Picasso and Braque walked round the object they were painting and put it all together in one picture. The two artists painted hundreds of cubist pictures.

Picasso then developed other styles, including neo-classicism, where he showed heaviness in pictures by making things look like they weighed a ton.

Then he began making sculpture out of rubbish. In 1943 he made a bull's head out of a bicycle saddle and handlebars.

Picasso painted another great picture, in 1937: Guernica. This was a mural (a painting on a wall) and it showed horror, pain, and great sadness — all the things that Picasso felt about the bombing of Guernica during the Spanish Civil War.

In 1955 Picasso moved to the South of France. He never stopped work, and made beautifully decorated pots, more paintings, sculptures, and thousands of drawings. He was very funny, which is why many of his paintings are funny. He made masks, and liked to wear brightly coloured trousers. He had several striped pairs of trousers made for him, but we don't know if he had stripy pants!

Picasso worked very hard every day, even the last day of his life. He was 92 when he died in his home in 1973. He'd made over 20,000 pieces of art.

"Every child is an artist. It's a challenge to remain an artist when you grow up." Pablo Picasso